Little Bunny's Lunch

Written by JoAnne Nelson ▪ Illustrated by Bari Weissman

 MODERN CURRICULUM PRESS

PROJECT DIRECTOR: **Judith E. Nayer**
ART DIRECTOR: **Lisa Lopez**

Published by Modern Curriculum Press

 Modern Curriculum Press, Inc.
A division of Simon & Schuster
13900 Prospect Road, Cleveland, Ohio 44136

This edition is published simultaneously in Canada by
Globe/Modern Curriculum Press, Toronto.

ISBN 0-8136-1120-2 (STY PK)   ISBN 0-8136-1117-2 (BK)

10 9 8 7 6 5   95 94 93

There go all the bunnies
in a **bunch, bunch, bunch,**
running to the garden
for their **lunch, lunch, lunch.**

"Yum, yum," said Little Bunny
with a crunch, crunch, crunch.
"I'll eat these orange carrots
for my **lunch, lunch, lunch.**"

"Yum, yum," said Uncle Bunny
with a **munch, munch, munch**.
"I'll eat this big white cabbage
for my **lunch, lunch, lunch**."

"Yum, yum," said Grandpa Bunny,
"I've a **hunch, hunch, hunch,**
I'll eat this round red radish
for my **lunch, lunch, lunch.**"

"Yum, yum," said Grandma Bunny
with a **scrunch**, **scrunch**, **scrunch**.
"I'll eat these purple turnips
for my **lunch**, **lunch**, **lunch**."

"Yum, yum," said Mama Bunny
with a crunch, crunch, crunch.
"I'll eat this fresh green lettuce
for my **lunch**, **lunch**, **lunch**."

8

"Stop, stop," said Uncle Bunny
with a shush, shush, shush.
"I think I hear some footsteps
in the **brush, brush, brush**."

"Run, run," said Grandma Bunny
with a **thump**, **thump**, **thump**.
And they rushed back to their tunnel
with a **jump**, **jump**, **jump**.

"Help, help," said Little Bunny
with a thud, thud, thud,
as he stumbled and then tumbled
in the **mud**, **mud**, **mud**.

"Come, come," said Mama Bunny
with a **hush**, **hush**, **hush**.
And they hurried home together
in a **rush**, **rush**, **rush**.

13

bump, bump, bump

"Oh, my," said Little Bunny
with a bump, bump, bump.
"There's a rumble in my tummy
and a **lump, lump, lump.**"

"Hush, hush," said Mama Bunny,
"I've a **hunch, hunch, hunch**,
you ate too many carrots
for your **lunch, lunch, lunch**."

"Shush, shush," said Mama Bunny
with a **hug**, **hug**, **hug**.
And she tucked him in his bed
where he was **snug**, **snug**, **snug**.